THE DRUG ABUSE PREVENTION LIBRARY

DRUGS AND ANGER

Bea O'Donnell Rawls

THE ROSEN PUBLISHING GROUP, INC.

NEW YORK

Published in 1995 by The Rosen Publishing Group, Inc.
29 East 21st Street, New York, NY 10010

Copyright 1995 by The Rosen Publishing Group, Inc.

First Edition

Library of Congress Cataloging-in-Publication Data

O'Donnell Rawls, Bea.
    Drugs and anger / Bea O'Donnell Rawls. — 1st ed.
        p.   cm. — (The Drug abuse prevention library)
    Includes bibliographical references and index.
    ISBN 0-8239-1706-1
    1. Youth—United States—Substance use—
Psychological aspects—Juvenile literature.
2. Substance abuse—United States—Psychological
aspects—Juvenile literature.   3. Anger—Juvenile
literature.   4. Stress in youth—United States—
Juvenile literature.   5. Stress management for
teenagers—Juvenile literature.   [1. Substance abuse—
Psychological aspects.   2. Anger.   3. Stress
(Psychology)   4. Stress management.]   I. Title.
II. Series.
HV4999.Y68036   1994
616.86'00835—dc20   94-1906
                                                      CIP
                                                      AC

Contents

Introduction *6*

Chapter 1 Turtle Lane to Juvie Hall *11*

Chapter 2 Why Me? *20*

Chapter 3 Sentencing *31*

Chapter 4 Good Anger and Bad Anger *38*

Chapter 5 The Power to Choose *51*

Glossary—Explaining New Words *57*

Help List *59*

For Further Reading *62*

Index *63*

Introduction

Young people seldom ask if there is a connection between drugs and anger. They probably think the two are entirely separate. In fact, sometimes there is a connection, and sometimes there isn't. It's possible to use drugs and not feel angry. It's also possible to get angry and not use drugs. A more important question is what can happen when an angry person uses drugs or alcohol.

Before we talk about the relationship between anger and using drugs and alcohol, it's important to understand the terms "using" and "drugs and alcohol."

Many teens don't realize the consequences of experimenting with drugs.

Alcohol makes you more likely to get into fights.

Drugs and alcohol means everything from legal over-the-counter or prescribed medications to illegal, mind-altering substances. Marijuana, crack, heroin, and alcohol are examples of illegal substances. Alcohol is an illegal drug for people under the age of 21.

Using can include anything from a single hit to "take two tablets after meals." *Using* can mean one social drink or drug or alcohol addiction.

A one-beer-a-night drinker might think the danger of mixing drugs with anger applies only to addicts or serious stoners. That is not the case.

Drugs and alcohol affect everyone differently. A person's body chemistry determines the effect. A person's size affects how the body reacts to drugs and alcohol. What a person has eaten and how long ago can affect how the body will react. A person's physical condition can affect the reaction, and so can a person's mental attitude.

It's important to know that both drugs and alcohol are mind-altering substances. They can affect how you act or react. They can be addictive. Addiction is a disease, and unless it is treated it will eventually kill you. An addict may die from the disease itself or from something related. A person killed in an auto accident while under the influence of drugs or alcohol is a victim of addiction. There is no way to know ahead of time if you will become addicted.

Drugs and alcohol have the power to change your life. Mixing drugs and anger is a sure way to change your life. This book tells the story of Michael, who mixed drugs, alcohol, and anger. It changed his life in ways he never dreamed could happen to him.

Alcohol and drugs can confuse your life.

CHAPTER 1

Turtle Lane to Juvie Hall

That awful Saturday was supposed to be the best day of my life. On Wednesday I turned 16. I got my driver's license on Thursday. It didn't get any better than turning 16, getting your license, and having a day off work. But it didn't turn out that way.

It had been two weeks since I'd had a day off work at Taco Bell. Those two weeks had been lousy. We had tests at school, and I didn't know the stuff.

Mom had to train a new cook at the nursing home where she worked. That meant I had to feed the little kids and get them to bed before I went to work. I was tired, and the kids were a pain in the butt. It seemed as if all I did was take care of them.

12 *But it was spring break and I had a day off. Me and my buddies decided to go to Turtle Lane to hang out. Mom's boyfriend was feeling generous, because he let me use his car. Kind of a birthday present, I guess.*

Turtle Lane was a great place to party. We had beer, and Steve brought some pot. Some girls showed up. I knew them from school and kind of liked Tess. We smoked a couple of joints and talked. I could tell she sort of liked me too. I had music, beer, a little pot, and a girl. Man, it was great.

Then a bunch of guys from another school showed up and started giving Tess and her friends a hard time, but the girls just blew them off. The turnoff must have made the guys mad. Well, Tess tells them to shove it, and one guy gets really mad. He grabs her and pushes her up against the car. He tells her he don't take nothing off a fat slob like her.

I tell him to chill out and leave her alone. He wants to know if I plan to make him. I go, "Yeah, if I have to," and give him a shove. The dude shoves me, and the next thing I know we're going at it. Then his buddies and my buddies get mixed up in it.

I don't really know what happened after the fight started. All I know is I was mad. This guy had no right coming on to Tess, no right shoving her around. He had no right messing with me and my buddies. He had no right screwing up my birthday. He had no right shoving me. So I hit him.

The more I hit him, the madder I got. All I could think of was how this was supposed to be the best day of my life, and he was screwing it up. So I kept on hitting him.

I didn't hear the cops come. Everybody was yelling and screaming. The cops pulled me off the guy. I started swinging at them. I kicked one of them and bit another.

The next thing I knew I was on my face in the dirt with my arms twisted behind me. I heard the handcuffs click when they snapped around my wrists.

My head was pounding. I heard people yelling and somebody crying. Then I heard the ambulance. At first I thought it was for me. I could feel blood on my face and I hurt everywhere. But the ambulance wasn't for me.

I heard someone say something about head injuries and a spleen. They were talking about the guy I was fighting with. They put him in the ambulance. Then I understood that I'd hurt him really bad, but I didn't care. In fact, I was glad. He shouldn't have messed with me.

I was mad at him and mad at the cops. I was mad at Tess for mouthing off at that guy.

14 | *I was mad at Mom for making me take care of the kids so much. I was mad because I did rotten in school. I was mad at myself. I was mad at life.*

We pulled out of Turtle Lane and headed for Juvie Hall.

Anger: What Is It?

Anger is a feeling. It starts in a person's mind as a thought or an idea. When it exists only in your mind, it is neither good nor bad. If a feeling or thought never left your mind, it would never be good or bad. How you *react* to what you think or feel can be good or bad. What you do or say can be called right or wrong.

Kids are often taught that angry feelings are bad. When they act angry, adults send them to their room "until you can come out and be nice." The message is that anger is bad. What adults really mean is that *violent reactions* to anger are not appropriate.

Moods

Anger is like many other feelings. Happy, sad, lonely, and grouchy all start in your mind. Other people know you are happy or sad by the way you act. People think you are happy when they see you laugh or smile

Your words, expressions, and actions show how you feel.

Some teenagers think smoking and drinking will help them fit in.

or whistle. Sad words and actions send a message that you are gloomy or down.

People understand your mood by what you do, how you look, and what you say. Happy thoughts result in positive, happy actions—a good mood. Angry thoughts result in negative, angry actions—a bad mood.

Michael was feeling happy on his birthday. He was excited about having a day off, having his driver's license, and being allowed to take the car. His brothers and sisters didn't bug him. He teased them in fun for a change. He hugged his mom. He talked to his mom's boyfriend instead of ignoring him.

To Michael's family and friends, he was in a good mood. His actions showed how he felt.

When he got in the fight, he was reacting to the way he felt. His angry thoughts became very clear. The anger was a result of his thoughts about how everything was coming down on him. He thought other people were messing up his life, so he acted as angry as he felt.

Stress
Michael had a lot of stress in his life. His mother was divorced, and she didn't

Stress can be caused by a variety of factors, from taking
a test to fighting with a friend to speaking in public.

have a very good job. Money was always **19** tight, so Michael had to work. He had to help take care of the kids. School was hard, especially when he was working so many hours and didn't like to study.

It didn't seem fair to Michael that he had so much responsibility when other kids didn't. It made him mad when he thought about it. When the pressure was really on, he turned to partying so he could feel happy for a little while. Booze and pot gave him a buzz and made life look a little better. But when he got sober, life hadn't changed and he got angry all over again.

Michael didn't understand that the influence of drugs and alcohol changed his way of dealing with anger that day at the lake. They took control, and he put another kid in the hospital.

Combining drugs, alcohol, and angry thoughts makes for a very explosive situation. Without them, Michael still would have been angry, but he might not have lost control.

Sitting in the back of the patrol car, Michael was not only angry, he was scared. He was 16 years old and on his way to jail. How could life get so tangled up?

CHAPTER 2

Why Me?

*They say there's a difference between Juvenile Hall and jail, but I'm telling you there is **no** difference when those doors shut and lock. I've never been so scared in my life. And I never felt more alone.*

I was in there five hours before Mom and her boyfriend could get me out. I had enough time to think about what had happened and get over being mad, but I didn't. How could I be in jail for defending Tess? I was right. That guy was wrong. I got a raw deal.

I always got the raw deal, and I was sick of it. Life wasn't fair. Other guys didn't have to work like I did. They didn't have to baby-sit all the time. If my old man hadn't run out on us, things would be different. I hated him for dumping us.

School wasn't any better. I wasn't a brain and I wasn't a jock, so I didn't fit in. The teachers never paid any attention to me. The vice principal had it in for me ever since I got busted for drinking at a football game. That wasn't fair either. I wasn't the only one with beer, but I was the only one he suspended. I didn't like him and he didn't like me.

I got madder and madder when I thought about all the times the cops stopped me for nothing. Just because my hair was long, they tried to bust me for stuff adults do all the time. Like the time they stopped me and Bill at two in the morning for no reason except we were driving at two in the morning. We closed Taco Bell that night; we were tired and in a hurry to get home. So we burned a little rubber. What's the big deal?

They call jail the "cooler." Maybe some people cool off there, but I didn't. I was ticked off and sick. When I threw up, it seemed like the end. I lay down on my bunk and cried. All I could think of was, "Why me?"

Stress

Michael's life was no different from most people's lives in one way. He had a lot of stress. Stress is normal. In fact, some stress is actually desirable. There is stress

22 | when you get a new boyfriend or girl-
friend, but it isn't bad stress. Winning an
award brings some stress with it, but
most people like that kind of stress.

Just as anger is neither good nor bad,
stress is neither good nor bad. How you
react to it makes it good or bad. Michael
reacted to stress by turning to drugs and
alcohol and letting his anger run wild.

Stress usually comes from one of three
sources: (1) it can come from the world
around you—*environmental*; (2) it can
come from your body—*physical*; or (3) it
can come from your mind or thoughts—
mental.

Environmental Stress
Environmental stress is very common.
Crowded, polluted, and noisy cities can
be dangerous; people live in fear of drive-
by shootings or neighborhood gangs.
People worry about violent weather such
as hurricanes or tornadoes. Families without jobs feel stress. Some families fight all
the time. Drug or alcohol abuse puts
huge stress on families.

Eddie
*Eddie's school has a fence around it. There
are security guards in the halls and metal*

You can always walk away from an argument.

detectors at the doors. Everybody has to sit in the auditorium until classes start instead of going to their lockers or walking in the halls. There have been too many fights and too many weapons. Eddie sits with his friends because he's afraid. Some kids make fun of him and spit on him when he walks by. He's afraid to say anything or do anything. He feels sick to his stomach every day as he walks up the school steps. The school environment causes his stress.

Physical Stress

The second cause of stress comes from your body. Growing unusually fast causes

24 stress to a person's body. Serious illness or accidents can cause stress. Not eating right causes stress to a person's body. Drugs and alcohol cause stress. They are dangerous substances that poison the body, so it must fight to keep health in balance.

Annie

When Annie was a baby she got a blood infection that settled in her leg. By the time she was 14 years old, she had been in the hospital 18 times and had surgery on her leg six times. The infected leg didn't grow as fast as the other and was two inches shorter. She walked on crutches. Her leg hurt all the time. Between the pain and feeling left out, Annie was tense. She had a short temper and found herself looking for something— anything—to make her feel better. It started with a beer. By the time Annie was 16 she was an alcoholic. She discovered that alcohol let her forget the physical stress for a while and took away the anger of feeling out of place. Now Annie had two major problems. Her life was in danger of com- ing apart, and that made her angry too. Annie was under serious physical stress.

Mental Stress

The third kind of stress comes from a person's thoughts. Telling yourself you're ugly, no good, fat, or dumb causes stress. Worrying about what others think about you causes stress. Wishing you looked like someone else causes stress. Thoughts that include *should, ought to, have to, must,* or *hate* usually cause stress. Thoughts are powerful, and they set the tone for how you feel.

Erica

Erica's dad drank a lot. When he got home from work he headed straight for the refrigerator and the beer. If he saw anything out of place, he started yelling. He called Erica ugly names. Neither Erica nor what she did was ever good enough. She grew up believing she was worthless and unlovable. Her father's behavior caused Erica mental stress.

Physical Reaction to Stress

All the stressful situations we've talked about and many others result in a physical reaction. Muscles get tense. Armpits and palms get clammy, cold, or sweaty. Eyes dilate. Throat gets tight. The voice gets higher. Stomach muscles cramp.

A parent's behavior can be the cause of stress.

Breathing gets faster or breath is short. Blood pressure rises.

These are some of the body's signals of stress. The signals get stronger as the stress level goes up. The body demands relief. If it doesn't get relief, illness usually results. Ulcers and headaches are common bodily reactions to high stress levels.

Behavioral Reactions to Stress
People react to stress in many ways, but each is an effort to escape stress. Some people withdraw. Others get sick or can't

Turning to drugs and alcohol is not a good way to deal with stress and anger.

sleep. Some people overeat; others bite their fingernails. Some laugh and pretend the stressful problems don't exist. This is called *denial*. Anger is a common behavioral reaction to stress. All of these reactions are methods of releasing the stress level so the body doesn't become ill.

A person's body is an early warning system: It tells the person to listen carefully because something is about to happen.

Events in your life that cause stress are

28 | unique to you. What stresses you may not stress someone else. Before you can control your reaction to stress, you need to know what causes stress for you.

Charts have been made of common stressful events. Often they deal with stress in adult lives, but many of the same things cause stress for young adults. Look for stress charts in the psychology section of your library.

Stress Chart for Young Adults

The following are common events that cause stress for anyone, but particularly for young adults. Read the list and write down the ones that apply to you. Think of other events that cause you to feel tense or nervous and add them to the list.

Death of a close family member or close friend

Divorce or separation

Major illness or injury

Moving to a new neighborhood

Changing schools and/or failing a class

Pregnancy

Trouble at school, at home, or with the law

Family arguments

Fights with friends
Not having enough money
Breaking up with a boyfriend or
  girlfriend
Not fitting in
Loss of a best friend
How you look
What others think of you.

Now that you have identified the big events that cause you stress, examine how your body reacted. Use the following scale to rate each stressful situation.

Body Signals

Beside each event on your list, check the level of anxiety or worry you felt on a scale of 1 to 10.

Uneasy   *Uncomfortable*   *Painful*
1   2   3   4   5   6   7   8   9   10

Notice how many events were 5 or above. What did your body tell you at those times? Did your face get red? Did your heart beat faster? Did your hands get sweaty? Did your muscles tighten? What are *your* body signals when you are feeling stress? Write them down.

Counselors can help you identify what kinds of stress you have in your life.

Reactions

Now think about what you *do* when your body sends stress signals. Do you get angry? Do you split so you don't have to face the situation? Do you whine or pout? Do you turn to drugs or alcohol? Do you argue or fight? Do you lose control?

Knowing the signals of stress and tension *before* you react gives you a chance to control what you do or say. You are forewarned and ready to be in charge.

CHAPTER 3

Sentencing

*T*he courtroom was clean. It smelled like lemon furniture polish. The wooden chairs shined and so did the windowsills. Every footstep echoed. The hair on my neck stood out, and I could feel my knees grind as I walked. The judge had gray hair and didn't look glad to see me. Everything seemed bigger and louder than real life. It was like a slow-motion movie. I didn't want to be there. But I was.

They read the charges against me. Assault and Minor in Possession. *This felt like something on television. It couldn't really be me in front of that sour-looking judge.*

The judge asked me a question. I was looking at my shoelaces trying to decide if the left one was going to break the next time I tied it. I didn't answer. She said something else and I went, "Huh?" That must have made her mad.

She goes, "Young man, look at me when you speak. You are here on very serious charges, and I want your full attention." That made me a little mad. Who did she think she was anyway?

She went through a pile of papers and talked to the guy from Juvie who came with me. They talked about me like I was a delinquent or something. Then she started asking me questions about times when I got caught shoplifting and when the cops broke up parties at my house. She even knew about trouble I'd been in at school. It didn't seem like any of her business, and I said so. I guess I sounded a little snotty because it made her really mad.

She goes, "Michael, do you realize the young man you beat up is in serious condition? Do you know that he may suffer permanent damage to his vision because you were drinking and out of control? Do you understand how much trouble you are in?"

I go, "Yeah, I guess."

Then she said something about this not being the first time I'd been in trouble for drinking and losing my temper. She said that I had to see a counselor to find out if I was an alcoholic and to help me get control of my temper.

I thought she was nuts. Me? An alcoholic? Maybe I was a little short-tempered, but I didn't need help from a counselor.

As it turned out, I didn't have any choice. She sentenced me to counseling for anger management and substance abuse. That day was really turning out to be the worst day of my life. The judge sentenced me. It sounded like I was a criminal. I felt like a criminal.

Michael went to see a drug and alcohol counselor. The counselor did an assessment and told Michael that he was addicted, but he didn't want to hear it or believe it. This is called *denial*.

Michael was assigned to a counseling group with eight other young people who all had similar problems: All of them had short tempers, and all of them used drugs and alcohol to deal with their anger.

The counselor worked with them on identifying the kinds of stress they had in their lives. He helped them learn how stress and tension need a release. He helped them discover how they reacted to stress. He helped them learn to listen to their bodies. He helped them learn to pay

34 | attention to the kinds of situations that set off angry reactions.

The next thing the group did was learn ways to avoid violent reactions that got them in trouble. They began by learning about physical ways to deal with anger.

Time-Out

One positive physical action you can take when you recognize conditions are right for you to get angry is to take a time-out. You stop what you are doing or thinking and get away for a period of time. You should take a time-out when your body begins to send warning signals about anger.

Taking a time-out is not as easy as it sounds. Old habits are hard to break. Sometimes you can't just get up and leave. If you are in class, walking out could upset the teacher. You could have *two* frustrating situations to deal with.

Some people are afraid that if they take a time-out their friends will think they are cowardly for walking away from a fight. Some like to get the last word.

A few rules can help you learn the time-out habit:

Communicate what you are going

to do. You might say, "I'm getting really mad. I'm taking a time-out so I don't do something I'll be sorry for." If people know what you are doing, they aren't as likely to misunderstand when you get up and walk away.

Leave the area. Make sure your time-out is long enough for you to get control and to give the other person a chance to cool off. Thirty minutes or more is best. Get completely away if possible.

Do not drink, use, or drive during your time-out. Never break this rule. If you are extremely angry, your mind won't be on driving, and that puts both you and others at risk. Drugs and alcohol make the situation worse.

Return only when you are in control. Your body signals will tell you when you're ready to deal with the situation.

Don't wait until you're in a flaming rage to try a time-out. Try practicing when you're only a little annoyed. A time-out works. Don't be afraid to try it.

Breathing Exercises

The physical signals of anger usually reduce the supply of oxygen to the blood. Signals such as tight muscles, shortness of breath, or a red face tell you that you

36 | are not breathing deeply. Deep breathing enables the body to get rid of impurities that add to the stress you already feel.

Controlling your breathing can be like a mini time-out. Concentrate on getting lots of fresh air in your system when it isn't possible to leave the scene. When you concentrate on breathing, your mind is focused on something other than what has upset you.

Breathing deeply takes a little practice, but it isn't hard. As you practice, pay attention to the spot on your body that moves when you breathe in and out. Learn to breathe from deep in your lungs. Short, shallow breaths come from the chest and don't provide much air. Make the spot just above your belt move.

Inhale through your nose. Hold the breath and count to five. Exhale slowly through your mouth. Do this for five or ten minutes, concentrating on the process. Within several deep breaths you will begin to feel relaxed.

When anger signals come, take several deep breaths to help you gain control. Taking ten deep breaths is a way of counting to ten when you are upset. Counting to ten is good advice.

Physical exercise is a good way to get rid of stress and anger.

Exercise

Get *physical* when you recognize your warning signals that stress levels are building. Run, walk, do push-ups, hit a punching bag, ride your bike, or scrub the tires on your car. Do something to burn up your anger-energy.

Exercise does two things for you: it creates a time-out, and it causes you to breathe deeply. So you use all three methods of taking control of your anger by doing something physical.

Michael's grouchy judge did him a favor. Instead of giving him time to serve for the assault charges, she sentenced him to learn healthy ways to deal with anger.

CHAPTER 4

Good Anger and Bad Anger

I gotta tell you I wasn't too hot about going to see a counselor. It embarrassed me. I was afraid my friends would think I was nuts or something. Only people with mental problems went to see a shrink. I did not have a mental problem.

The first time I went, this guy talked for a long time. He must have asked me a million questions. He wanted to know everything from what I ate to whether my grandfather had diabetes. At first I thought he was just nosy. Then I found out that he was doing an Assessment. *All those questions helped him figure out if I had a problem with drugs and alcohol. That guy really knew what he was doing, but I didn't trust him at first.*

38

Nelson Mandela is an example of good anger. He channeled
his anger to the fight against the system of apartheid,
oppression of black South Africans, and won. He is now the
President of South Africa.

40

He told me how addiction was a disease. He said I shouldn't feel guilty about having a disease, but I did at first. He said it wasn't going to be easy to get well.

When I first started going to Group, I didn't talk much. I only answered when someone asked me a question. I didn't plan to get into that personal stuff, but I did a lot of listening.

Pretty soon I found out the others in Group were a lot like me. They were getting in trouble because they were using and because they had bad tempers.

After he taught us about listening to our bodies, he told us about good anger and bad anger and helped us figure out which was which. We learned how to think differently about what made us mad. That was the hardest part.

I hate to admit it, but I got to like Group. It was good not to feel so alone. Other kids had it tough too. I got to like the idea that my life could get better. If I could figure out the difference between good anger and bad anger, maybe—just maybe . . .

Good Anger Reactions

Michael's counselor described good anger as a feeling that comes from something that's unfair, unjust, and hurts people.

Good anger is good only if it makes people do something positive to correct a bad situation.

In 1955 a woman named Rosa Parks practiced good anger. She refused to give up her seat on the bus because she was black. It wasn't right to be treated like a second-class citizen. Rosa Parks practiced good anger and helped the civil rights movement begin.

The Reverend Martin Luther King Jr. led the movement with passive resistance. People were angry about the injustice of segregation. They fought injustice without violence. They challenged injustice with peace marches. They rejected injustice in court.

This is an example of good anger. People took positive actions to help correct a bad situation.

Bad Anger Reactions

Bad anger, on the other hand, can be about something that should be changed, but negative actions are taken to change it. The Los Angeles riots following the Rodney King trial are an example. A bad anger reaction is not productive even when something serious needs to be changed. War, killing, and race riots are

The riots in Los Angeles in 1992 are an example of bad anger. The riots caused the destruction of a city. Millions of dollars worth of damage was done to businesses and homes, many of which are not restorable.

really serious bad-anger reactions that only make matters worse.

Both good anger and bad anger reactions start in your mind. Now we're back to talking about anger as a thought. The thought is neither good nor bad. It is your reaction to it that is good or bad.

Listening to Your Thoughts

Just as you have learned to listen to your body when it tells you something is making you mad, you can learn to listen for the kinds of thoughts that upset you.

Begin to listen to the talk in your

mind. These silent conversations you have with yourself often cause stress and trigger angry reactions. Self-talk is frequently negative. Controlling negative thoughts helps you to control stress, your temper, and sometimes the situation. Michael learned that controlling his thinking is a part of anger management.

Self-Talk

People act the way they think. People with happy thoughts act happy. Thinking is self-talk. Listening to self-talk will help you understand your reactions in situations that make you angry.

There is a pattern to self-talk. It goes like this:

Something happens. *Maria's bus is caught in traffic. There was an accident on the freeway. She is late to work. When she gets there, her boss yells, "You're late!"*

Maria's self-talk might sound like this. *"That S.O.B. hates me. She's going to fire me. It was my fault because I should have taken an earlier bus."*

Maria's body reacts. *Her face turns red. Her stomach begins to hurt. Her throat gets dry, and her hands shake.*

Maria reacts. *The girl working next to her smiles. Maria says, "What are you grin-*

44 | *ning about, stupid? Someday I'm going to give that witch a piece of my mind."* Maria *is rude to customers and breaks two cups.* Her thinking is filled with angry self-talk and she acts angry.

Learning about Your Own Self-Talk

Self-talk is usually patterned after what you saw as you were growing up. When adults are calm and kind, kids learn about being calm and kind. If adults are violent and mean, kids learn about being violent and mean. Ideas about how to act set the tone for your self-talk.

Self-talk happens so fast that sometimes you don't realize it's going on. It's important to recognize self-talk. Thoughts give signals to your mind about how you are reacting before you start *acting* angry. You can control how you act when you know how you think. Remember: You act the way you think.

Three kinds of self-talk are typical of thinking that leads to anger: labeling, mind reading, and overstating. All of them lead to negative thinking.

Labeling

Calling names is a form of labeling. Maria called her boss an s.o.b. and the girl working next to her stupid. When people label others, they stop thinking about the person and start thinking about a label. It's easier to be angry with a label than a person. Maria got mad at the s.o.b., not her boss named Elaine. Name-calling or labeling fuels anger like dry grass on a campfire.

Mind Reading

Mind reading is *assuming* that you know what another person is thinking. Maria was mind reading when she assumed that Elaine hated her. She had no way to know what Elaine really thought, so she made it up in self-talk. She called the girl next to her stupid, *assuming* the girl was smiling about the boss yelling at her.

With mind reading, you are guessing that others think the same way you do. Your self-talk may be what *you* think but is probably not what someone else is thinking. You may be giving someone else your negative thoughts.

Overstating

This kind of self-talk makes things bigger than they really are. Maria's self-talk made things worse than they really were. Elaine yelled that Maria was late; she did

46 | not mention firing. Overstating tends to make anger worse because you think the worst.

Dealing with Self-Talk

Taking control of your self-talk is not easy, but it is not impossible. Start listening to it. Do you hear yourself calling others names (*labeling*) when you're ticked off at them? Do you hear yourself expecting the worst (*overstating*)? Do you think you know what someone else is thinking (*mind reading*)?

Write It down

If you are serious about breaking negative self-talk habits, start writing it down each time you hear yourself using it. Keep a log or a diary for at least two weeks to start. You will soon notice what kinds of situations start your negative self-talk.

As you log your self-talk, notice your body reactions. Soon you will begin to recognize body signals that go with negative self-talk. Now you have two signals (body signals and self-talk) that can warn you when anger is just around the corner. This is called *awareness*. Once you know what to watch for, you are

Writing down your feelings can help you deal with anger and stress.

48 | ready to learn new ways to act when the signals come. Awareness is the first step in changing a habit. It takes work, but there are a few tricks that can help.

Substitute

Each time you hear yourself labeling someone, stop. Use the name. If you're mad at someone you don't know, make up a name. Call the person Sarah or Sam.

Do a reality check. Are you using a real name or a label? Does your self-talk make the situation bigger than it really is?

"That jerk deserves to die," is an example of both labeling and overstating. Give the person a name. Describe the real situation. The truth is that Joe (the jerk) broke a date with you. You have a right to be upset, but Joe doesn't deserve to die for standing you up. It's harder to be mad at Joe than at a jerk.

Measure

Check your self-talk for accuracy. Is Joe's breaking a date the worst thing that could happen to you? It may hurt, but you could name hundreds of worse things. Self-talk can throw your thinking out of balance. Overstating makes a bad situation worse.

Listen

Just as you listen to self-talk, listen to what others are saying. Listen without making judgments. Listen to the words used. Ask questions if you don't understand. Listen for what people mean. Sometimes what they say isn't what they really mean. Listening takes practice, and it takes time. But being a good listener prevents mind reading.

Talk

Tell others what you are feeling. Avoid using the word *you*. Instead, concentrate on the words *I feel* or *I felt*.

Let's go back to the date Joe broke. When you talk to Joe, tell him how you felt. "I felt *angry* the night you broke the date with me. It made me feel *sad* because I was *afraid* you didn't like me anymore." Those words tell Joe how you felt. Telling Joe he was a scum for standing you up would make him mad, and communication would stop. Telling him how you feel helps communication. It keeps the yelling down, the blood pressure down, and tempers under control.

50 | ### *Write*

If you don't feel comfortable talking about how you feel, try writing a letter about your feelings, but don't send it right away. Read it later to see if you were clear and still feel the same way. If it isn't accurate, rewrite it. When it is clear, send it. This method gives the other person time to think about your feelings before you start to talk.

In Summary

Michael learned a lot about anger management in Group. He learned that it's hard to change old habits, but he learned new methods to do it. He learned a lot about himself. He learned that control is about *reactions* to anger, not about what causes it.

The Power to Choose

It was late when the telephone rang. I had just gotten the kids to bed. Steve was on the other end.

"Hey, big guy. Do I gotta a deal for you! We're gonna party down at the lake after graduation. Look out, Turtle Lane! Mitch is getting a keg and it's going to be a real blow-out. Who knows when all of us may be able to get together again? Did you know Randy's going in the Navy in two weeks and Rich is heading for Alaska to fish with his uncle? Tess will be there, but she's bringing her dweeb boyfriend. It'll only cost you five bucks for the keg and you got all the beer you can hold. What do you say? Count you in?"

As I listened, I could see the whole party in my mind. We'd have a big fire and Mitch

You can choose to avoid drugs and alcohol.

would have the keg in the back of his truck.
*Randy and Chris would make out. Tina
would dance after she had a few beers. Jay
would keep everybody laughing, and Jed
would just drink and watch. Holly would
flirt with everybody. It would be fun, all
right. And it was graduation.*

*Then I flashed to the last two years I'd
spent going to Group. The last thing the drug
and alcohol counselor told us was that we
had the power to choose. He was right. I
could choose to party hard. I could choose to
go and be the designated driver. I could
choose not to go. I could choose anything I
wanted.*

*"Yeah, man. This is the big one, and I
don't have to work the next day. You say
Mitch is getting a keg?"*

*"Beer on tap and hard stuff too, if you
want it. Tim will have something to smoke.
He always does. Man, I can't wait."*

*I thought of those handcuffs. I thought of
the fun it would be down at the lake. I
thought about how I was going to miss all
those guys next year. I thought about the
power to choose.*

*"Sounds great. Listen, I'll get back to
you. I got a couple of things I gotta check
out, but I'll let you know. OK?" I hung up
the phone and thought, "Yep, I do have the*

54 | *power to choose. I can do whatever I want to do."*

    It felt good.

The Power to Choose

Michael served his sentence by going to group counseling to learn about anger management. It was hard. He had a lifetime of negative self-talk habits to unlearn. He learned about listening for signals from his body.

He discovered how explosive it was to add drugs and alcohol to his temper problems. It didn't take long to see that that combination was as dangerous as drinking and driving.

Michael's most important discovery was that people own the power to choose. It is an act you practice almost every minute of every day. Some of the choices you make are small, and you don't think much about them. Other choices are huge and can affect the rest of your life. Michael had a hard time believing that the power really belonged to him.

Slowly he began to realize that he could control his life. He could choose to react to situations any way he wanted. Others might put demands on him, but he could choose how to react.

Using the power to choose means accepting the fact that what comes next also belongs to you. If your mother asks you to do something, you can choose to do it or not. If you choose not to do it, you are choosing what comes next. Mom will react. She might yell at you or ground you. But *you* get to make the first choice. You decide whether you'd rather have your mother yell at you or do what she asks.

You have the power to direct your self-talk. You decide how to react to your body signals. If you act the way you think and you have the power to choose what you think, you are in control.

The power to choose carries a price. You can choose what you want, but you also have responsibility for the result. You determine whether the *result* is something you really care about.

Accepting the responsibility for what happens to you is a giant step in growing up. It's much easier to blame someone else for what happens than to accept the responsibility for your choices. It's far better to be in control of your own life than to let someone else make choices for you.

No one can take away your power to

56 | choose unless you let them. Hang on to it. It's yours. It's your single most important tool in managing your life. It lets you make life happen. Life doesn't happen to you. You are in the driver's seat.

Michael went to the refrigerator and got a can of Pepsi. He popped the top, flipped on the TV, put his feet up on the coffee table, and took a long swallow. He thought about the party on graduation night. It sounded like a lot of fun. He smiled to himself and thought about it. He could decide to do whatever he wanted. He was in control because he had the power to choose.

It really felt good.

Glossary
Explaining New Words

addiction Dependence on drugs or alcohol.

alcoholic Person who suffers from the disease of alcoholism. An alcoholic has lost the ability to control the use of alcoholic beverages.

assault Verbal or physical threat that results in physical harm or the fear of physical harm.

assessment Evaluation tool used to determine if a person has a problem with drugs or alcohol.

bad anger Anger that causes negative or damaging actions.

denial Refusal to admit that one has a problem.

drug and alcohol counselor—Person specially trained in treatment of alcohol or drug abuse.

good anger—Anger that results in positive actions intended to correct a problem.

58 | **group**—Regularly scheduled meetings of
people in treatment or counseling for a
similar problem.

joint—Street name for a marijuana
cigarette.

Juvie or Juvenile Hall—Detention
center especially designed to deal with
youthful offenders.

minor in possession—Underage person
found with illegal drugs or alcohol.

stress—Reaction to a mental, physical,
or environmental situation that results
in an uncomfortable feeling in the
mind or body.

Help List

Most telephone books list numbers for organizations devoted to helping people in need. These organizations usually can tell you where to get help for problems not directly connected to substance abuse. Talk to a family member, a school counselor, or a trusted adult friend.

The following organizations have people who will talk to you. They will not tell anyone what you say. They will tell you where you can go for more help.

If the number begins with 1-800, there is no charge for the phone call. The other numbers do have a long-distance charge. DO NOT call a 1-900 number for help; trustworthy services do not use 1-900 numbers.

Alateen

This is a support group for teenagers who have a family member who is an alcoholic. If there is no listing for Alateen, call the number for AA (Alcoholics Anonymous) and ask if there is a nearby Alateen group.

AA (Alcoholics Anonymous)
Many have a 24-hour hotline number.
CA (Cocaine Anonymous)
1-213-559-5833
Cocaine Baby Hotline
1-800-327-BABE (in Illinois, Indiana, Kentucky, Michigan, Minnesota, Missouri, or Wisconsin.) 1-312-908-0867 (in other states)

DA (Drugs Anonymous)
1-212-874-0700 (New York area)
Drug and Alcohol Hotline
1-800-252-6465
National Council on Alcoholism and Drug Dependency
1-800-NCA-CALL, or
1-800-622-2255

Ethnic-Oriented Services

Calix Society
1-612-546-0544

This Catholic society sponsors support groups for recovering alcoholics.

Indian Health Service (IHS)

Regional programs to help Native Americans and Alaskan Natives with drug and alcohol treatment.

Alaska	1-907-257-1652
Arizona	1-602-241-2170
California	1-916-978-4191
Minnesota	1-218-751-7701
Montana	1-406-657-6944
New Mexico	1-505-552-6634
Oklahoma	1-405-231-5181
Oregon	1-503-221-4138
South Dakota	1-605-226-7456
Tennessee	1-615-736-5104 x35

Institute on Black Chemical Abuse (IBCA)
1-312-663-5780
Jewish Alcoholics, Chemically Dependent Persons and Significant Others (JACS)
1-212-473-4747

National Asian Pacific Families Against Abuse
1-301-530-0945
National Coalition of Hispanic Health and Human Services
1-202-371-2100

Help Services for Related Problems
Child Help USA
1-800-4-A-CHILD, or 1-800-422-4453
National Runaway Hotline
1-800-231-6946
1-800-392-3325 (Texas only)

In Canada, write or call:
Alcohol and Drug Dependency Information and Counseling Services (ADDICS)
#2,2471 $^1/_2$ Portage Avenue
Winnepig, MB R3J 0N6
204-831-1999

Narcotics Anonymous
P.O. Box 7500
Station A
Toronto, ON M5W 1P9
416-691-9519

Alcoholics Anonymous
#502, Intergroup Office
234 Enlington Avenue E.
Toronto, ON M4P 1K5
416-487-5591

For Further Reading

Black, Claudia. *It Will Never Happen to Me*. New York: Ballantine, 1987.

Coffee, Wayne. *Straight Talk about Drinking: Teenagers Speak Out*. New York: New American-Dutton, 1988.

Davis, Martha; Eshelman, Elizabeth R.; McKay, Mathew. *The Relaxation & Stress Reduction Workbook*. Oakland: New Harbenger Publications, 1982.

Edwards, Gabrielle I. *Coping With Drug Abuse*, rev. ed. New York: Rosen Publishing Group, 1990.

————. *Drugs on Your Streets*. New York: Rosen Publishing Group, 1991.

Luhn, Rebecca R. *Managing Anger*. Los Altos: Crisp Publications, Inc., 1992.

Rawls, Bea O'Donnell; Gwen Johnson. *Drugs and Where to Turn*. New York: Rosen Publishing Group, 1993.

Seixas, Judith S. *Drugs: What They Are, What They Do*. New York: William Morrow and Co., 1991.

Snyder, Anne. *My Name Is Davy. I'm an Alcoholic*. New York: New American-Dutton, 1986.

Index

A

accuracy, self-talk, 48–49
actions, negative, 17
addiction, disease of, 9, 40
alcohol, 8, 19, 33, 35
   and stress, 24
alcoholic, 24
anger
   dealing with, 19
   defined, 14
   good vs. bad, 40–42
   relation to drugs, 6
   and stress, 27
anger management, 33, 43, 54
attitude, mental, 9
awareness, 46–47

B

beer, 12, 21, 24, 25, 53
body chemistry, 9
body signals
   of anger, 34, 54
   of negative self-talk, 46
   reactions to, 30, 55
   of stress, 26, 27
   on stress chart, 29
breakup, romantic, 29
breathing exercises, 35–36, 37

C

choose, power to, 51–56
control
   learning, 54
   losing, 19
counselor, drug and alcohol,
   32–33, 38–40, 53
court appearance, 31–33

D

death, 28
denial, 27, 33
diary, self-talk, 46
divorce, 28
drugs, 8, 33, 35
   and anger, 6
   and stress, 24

E

exercise, 37

F

feeling
   anger as, 14
   reaction to, 17
fight, physical, 12–14, 29

G

girlfriend, defending, 12, 20
group counseling, 33, 40, 54

H

heroin, 8
home, problems at, 11–12,
   28

I

illness, 26, 28

K

King, Martin Luther Jr., 41
King, Rodney, 41

L

labeling, 44–45, 46, 48
listening, importance of, 49

M

marijuana, 8, 12, 19
mind reading, 45, 46
money problems, 29
moods, as feelings, 14–17
moving, 28

64

O
overstating, 45–46, 48

P
Parks, Rosa, 41
passive resistance, 41
pregnancy, 28

R
reactions, stress
 behavioral, 26–28
 good and bad anger, 40–42
 physical, 25–26
reaction, violent, 14, 34
responsibility, 19, 55
riots, Los Angeles, 41

S
school
 changing, 28
 problems in, 21, 32
 stress in, 22–23
self-talk, 43–50, 55
 negative, 54
 pattern of, 44

stress
 chart, 28–29
 desirable, 21
 environmental, 22
 identifying, 33–34
 mental, 22, 25
 physical, 22, 23–24
 reactions to, 22, 33
substance
 abuse, 33
 mind-altering, 9

T
thought
 anger as, 42, 44
 listening to one's, 42–43
 as stressor, 25
time-out, 34, 37

U
using, defined, 8–9

W
withdrawal, under stress, 26

About the Author

Bea O'Donnell Rawls is Dean of Academic and Technical Instruction at Rogue Community College, Grants Pass, Oregon. She was previously Director of Outreach Programs. She currently also works with local, regional, and state organizations that deal with educational reform in Oregon.

Ms. Rawls was a school counselor for nineteen years prior to her tenure at Rogue Community College. She worked with students and families with substance abuse problems in addition to advising students on career decisions and continuing education. She has also taught English, speech, and journalism.

Photo Credits

Cover photo: © Maje Waldo
Photos on pages 39, 42 © AP/Wide World Photos; all other photos: © Lauren Piperno